NUNCHAKU
Dynamic Training

D1557138

NUNCHAKU

Dynamic Training
Hirokazu Kanazawa

Published by

dragon books

Acknowledgements

Publisher	David Chambers
Translation	Yumiko Yokoma
Photography	Malcolm Copp-Taylor
Layout & Design	Garry O'Keefe, B.A. (Hons.)
Assistant	Mr. Yamada
U.S. Distributor	Sakura Dragon Corporation
Printed and bound by	Anchor Brendon Ltd, Tiptree, Essex.

Copyright © Dragon Books 1982

First printed September 1982
Seventh impression May 1985

ISBN No. 0 946062 01 3 L.C.C.C. No. 82-71144

Contents

Historical Background
Okinawan Martial Arts

Victory in the battle of Sekigahara in 1600 put General Tokugawa Iyeyasu in a position to finish the work of his predecessor, Oda Nobunaga and complete the unification of the Japanese Empire. At the same time to install himself as the first of a long line of Tokugawa Shogun (generalissimo) who would rule over a relatively peaceful Japan until the American, Commodore Perry, lifted the bamboo curtain of self-imposed seclusion in 1853.

To successfully rule a country as diverse and volatile as the Japanese archipelago, demanded a system of government so rigid that insurrection was unthinkable and impractical. Rules and regulations were the central feature of life under the Tokugawa Shogun. Laws were passed regulating the mode of dress, standards of behaviour and politics of all social classes, and were rigidly enforced by the officials of the Bakufu Government.

Even the Samurai, the elite of Tokugawa society were strictly controlled. The flamboyance of previous eras was frowned upon, and rules governing the length, style and decoration of their badge of office, the two swords thrust through their waistband, came thick and fast.

Contemporary records tell us that, in the 14th year of Keicho (1609 A.D.) the

Armed only with his kobudo weaponry, a peasant farmer lies in wait for his heavily armed samurai adversary.
An original Japanese woodblock print believed to be by the celebrated artist Yoshitoshi.

(Print owned by R.H. Clarke)

Lord of the Shimazu Han in Kyushu, Japan's southernmost island, was appointed governor of the Okinawan islands. Yet records cannot confirm the widely held belief that the confiscation of all edged weapons by the new political masters, and edicts that forbade ownership of the same, gave rise to the development of unarmed and farm implement fighting systems, that were the foundations of those that we have today.

Despite in depth research by students of martial arts history, (Hoplology) no contemporary record of such legislation has yet been found. Considering the fact that even such minor regulations as those governing the colour of a samurai's undergarments were scrupulously recorded, we can only regard this as one possible theory for the upsurge of native Okinawan martial arts, unless records are found to confirm this.

A more likely explanation, is the importation of martial skills from other Asian countries as a result of foreign trade and their adaptation by the Okinawans for their own use. It is a well known fact that ships from China and elsewhere visited Okinawan ports regularly. For according to the Master Funakoshi Gichin, founder of modern karate, Shiodaira of Shuri stated over 150 years ago that a Chinese expert, Ku Shanku visited the island with a group of his students and introduced a type of Kempo, and that noted Okinawan experts Gushi, Sakiyama and Tomoyori from the town of Naha, studied with the Chinese military attache.

Until the beginning of this century, the Okinawan martial arts were practised if not in secret, then in private; until in 1906 Funakoshi Gichin toured Okinawa with a group of friends giving public demonstrations. They later went on to give the first demonstration of Karate Do outside Okinawa, in 1916 at the Butoku-den in Kyoto the headquarters of the Japanese martial arts.

It is an endorsement of the faith that these old masters had in their art, that the modern world, both oriental and occidental, has enthusiastically embraced the way of Karate, and where it has gone so Kobudo has followed.

Samurai Field Marshal (1597)

Hirokazu Kanazawa
About the Author

Jan 1955 Kanazawa and friends outside Takushoku University Karate training hall.

As a young man, Hirokazu Kanazawa witnessed an Okinawan neighbour, not known as a martial artist, subdue in seconds a burly judo fifth dan who was trying to restrain him. He vowed on the spot to study this remarkable art that had impressed him so much, and thus began the karate career of Hirokazu Kanazawa, twice All Japan kata and kumite champion, senior International instructor and one of the greatest teachers of karate that the post war world has seen.

Enrolled by his parents in a university in Tokyo to study the family business of fishery, he transferred without telling them to Takushoku Univeristy as theirs was the karate club that he wanted to join. To maintain the subterfuge, he continued to wear the uniform of his original college on his visits home. The first that his parents knew of the change in their son's life, was when they read of his prowess at karate in a newspaper article.

At Takushoku University, the karate class was always oversubscribed. Students overflowed into the courtyard and practice in the dojo was often dangerous as over one hundred students kicked and punched with full power but less than total accuracy. In desperation, the organisers decided to reduce the numbers by making all students run to a local temple before every training session, dropping the last two to return from the club register. As the numbers dropped, so the fitness of the remaining students improved dramatically!

As a new student, remembers Master Kanazawa, life in the dojo was very hard. Nobody would dare mention how cold it was during the harsh Japanese winter for fear of being told to "practice until you warm up", a euphemism for training until you dropped. Being new to karate, he had to train harder than the other students to catch up. And so, for five or six hours every day, including a session from twelve midnight to 2am, the youthful Kanazawa forced himself towards his first black belt, which he attained after eighteen months at the age of twenty.

Graduation day was approaching as his university career came to its natural conclusion. Kanazawa had already been offered a good job with a company in Tokyo, and was looking forward to life in a successful business undertaking, as were so many of his contemporaries. Here fate played a hand in his future, for from no lesser person than Nakayama Sensei, chief instructor of the Japan Karate Association, came the offer of a position with his world renowned instructors class. All commercial aspirations abandoned, Kanazawa entered the JKA and applied himself to the training with a fury that would have done credit to the vandals that sacked ancient Rome.

As his technique improved, so he was encouraged to train harder and harder, the better he became the greater the incentive to improve. So year in year out, through diligent training, he forged the technique, dedication and fighting spirit for which he would soon become famous and which would make him a legend in his own lifetime. This improvement did not go unnoticed by his seniors. Kanazawa shone as a star amongst a class of star instructors all of whom would go on to become household names in later years in the countries to which they were assigned as chief instructors. All the seniors were agreed, this would be the man that they would train for the forthcoming, first All Japan Championship; the man to represent the JKA. The man they could not allow to fail.

As the decision of the seniors became public, Kanazawa was a marked man, a target for any young karate hopeful who wanted to make a name for himself by beating the star fighter of the JKA. Many tried but none succeeded. Thus in an atmosphere of intense speculation, he remained the favourite to win the coveted title and stepped up his training with only one thought in mind; the championship that he had to win at all costs. Many thought that the event would become a bloodbath as a result of the fanatical rivalry between schools, all realised the need for stringent refereeing and strict discipline. With four days to go, training was increased yet again to bring him to his peak.

During one of the full power battles that typified this last stage of his preparation, he realised that all was not well, his arm was troubling him, a pain just above the right wrist was spoiling his concentration. The doctor's verdict shook him, the arm was broken, there was no possibility of his fighting, favourite or not he would have to wait until next year for his chance at the championship. He returned to the JKA, the plaster cast on his right arm told the whole story, he could not fight, it would be too dangerous, he would try again next year. The words of the doctor rang in his ears like the peals of a giant bell as he made his lonely way back to the tiny Tokyo apartment that he called home.

There to his amazement waited his mother. She had made the long journey from the family home in Iwate Prefecture to see her son fight in the first All Japan Championship. How could he tell her now, after her long journey that he would not be competing. Seeing his right arm in plaster, and sensing the heaviness of her son's heart, she waited, saying nothing. "Mother" said Kanazawa, "the doctor has told me not to fight because my arm is broken". With the dignity inherited from her samurai forebears she replied.

"Tell me my son, do you practice karate with only one arm?"

"No mother, with the whole body."

"Then my son, you will fight!"

The day of the championship arrived, the stadium was packed with people, alone in the audience sat Kanazawa's mother, anxiously waiting to see her son compete. With no thought of winning he fought each opponent with great courage and skill. He recalls that their attacks although fierce and well timed, seemed to come at him in slow motion. He reached the quarter finals,

then the finals, suddenly to his great surprise he was being acclaimed by the audience as the first All Japan Karate Champion. In the crowd the old lady smiled to herself, she was proud of her son, and his triumph over hardship and pain, he was a good son she reminded herself.

The following year, this time at the peak of fitness he again won both the kata and kumite championships, but this time it was harder he remembers, with his title to defend. The attacks of his opponents came at him like bolts of lightning, he resolved to train even harder for the next championships. 1959 saw him lose the title as a result of a technical decision, but he was awarded a special prize for fighting spirit that had been reserved for the first competitor to win the championship in three consecutive years. A fitting reward for a man maturing from a first class championship fighter, into a teacher who would in years to come, set the standard for technique and performance of kata in the many countries that he visited as chief international instructor for the JKA.

Many instructors, having reached this elevated position at such a young age, would have rested on their laurels and enjoyed the accolades of their followers and colleagues. Not so Kanazawa, he trained still harder every day, incorporating the Chinese art of Tai Chi into his schedule under the tutelage of Mr. Yang. He also developed an interest in Okinawan weapons training (Kobudo) that led to the development of his own

Jan 1955 Training in the snow at the Takushoku University Headquarters.

system of nunchaku training and the publication of this book.

Drawing from the methods of the ancient Okinawan masters, his own background in classical karate and the techniques of several of the old schools of Japanese swordsmanship; he has developed a method that offers an effective system of self defence, a way of improving timing, reactions, and basic karate technique, and through the unique kata "Ju Ho", a method of improving health and well being. The study of this fascinating weapon following the method of this renowned instructor, whether as an interest in itself, or as part of a classical karate training programme, will without doubt, prove to be a rewarding and beneficial one.

A modest and immensely likeable man, Master Kanazawa lives in Tokyo with his wife and three sons, and continues to travel for six months of the year to teach students in thirty eight countries.

Nagatoro Japan 1955

Photographed at the end of a non-stop thirteen hour training hike, the Takushoku University Karate Club of the day contained many talented instructors destined to become internationally famous. Foremost among them, M. Nakayama and H. Nishiyama (2nd row, 3rd and 4th from right), K. Enoeda (3rd row, 3rd from left) and the author H. Kanazawa (front row centre).

徹
夜
行
脚

拓殖大学空手部

Introduction
Ryukyu Kobudo

For whatever reason the Okinawans were deprived of their weapons, they did not stay defenceless for long. The inhabitants of the Okinawan Islands devoted themselves, not only to the study of the unarmed fighting techniques that were originally imported from China, and would one day form the basis for modern Karate, but took up their everyday tools and utensils in defence of their lives and property.

By combining the basic movements of the unarmed systems, with the capabilities of the tools they knew so well from their daily labours, a wide range of closely related systems were developed by the peasant class, that we know today by the name Ryukyu Kobudo (Ryukyu=Okinawa Ko=ancient Budo=Martial Arts).

In those ancient times, only the insanely brave or reckless gambled with their lives by defying the prohibition on carrying weapons. Commonsense therefore dictated that the implements chosen by the peasants for self defence should not be regarded as weapons as such, should not seem suspicious or threatening, nor cause alarm. Thus the farmer chose his flail or sickle, the fisherman his paddle, so armed with the tools of his trade he could travel freely and without hindrance, few realising that the apparently unarmed peasant could

crush a skull or decapitate an armed man with his crude tools, while the fisherman was capable of despatching an assailant to the next world with his simple wooden paddle.

And so for centuries, under condition of extreme secrecy, the twin arts of armed and unarmed combat went hand in hand, or as I prefer to see them co-existed as the two wheels of the same cart, separate from each other, yet equally necessary if progress is to be made. Spiritually and historically joined, they are the twin planets in the galaxy of systems that we now refer to as the Okinawan martial arts. Contemporary masters would study all the disciplines, regarding them as individual segments of a complete fighting method.

The distancing of karate from the other arts, if this is the correct way of describing what happened, came about as a result of its introduction into mainland Japan by the noted Okinawan expert Funakoshi Gichin. Exposed to the influence of the purely Japanese martial arts such as Kendo and Judo, it was developed and polished along the same lines until it acquired a similar status to these ancient and highly respected disciplines, and took its place beside them. The arts involving the use of traditional weaponry did not however make such a successful crossing to the mainland. Okinawan masters that followed in the wake of Funakoshi Gichin to spread the seeds of knowledge of karate found that those relating to Ryukyu Kobudo fell almost entirely upon stony ground. The mainland Japanese while developing an almost insatiable appetite for knowledge of the new unarmed method, regarded fighting with any lesser weapons that the incomparable Japanese sword, or elegant long bow as demeaning, and an insult to their samurai ancestors, despite the fact that the majority were descended from peasants who, until the middle of the 19th century, lived in terror of the warrior class.

The past twenty years however have seen an upsurge of interest in these fascinating arts involving the use of traditional weapons. Students of karate have probed the connections between the disciplines, and come to realise the benefits in improved co-ordination and precise timing that serious study of these arts can develop. I feel strongly that as interest grows in the nunchaku, world wide, the day is not too far distant when this ancient and at one time almost forgotten art, will take its place beside Karate Do, its modern international cousin.

Daimyo-Feudal Baron (1600)

Kamae
The Stances

Rei no Kamae
Formal Stance

Musubi Dachi

Stand upright and relaxed, nunchaku in the left hand.

'Ready' position, all movements begin with this stance.

Yoi no Kamae
Preparatory Stance

Musubi Dachi

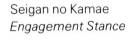

Seigan no Kamae
Engagement Stance

Renoji Dachi

Face your opponent gripping both batons
firmly in the forward hand.

Basic stance from which defensive and
attacking moves can be made.

Chudan Yama Kamae
Mountain Stance

Renoji Dachi

Shiho Kamae
Square Stance

Kokutsu Dachi

The 'square' block from which retaliatory
strikes can quickly be made.

Gyaku Shiho Kamae
Reverse Square Stance

Kokutsu Dachi

Gyaku Shiho Kamae
Reverse Square Stance

Neko Ashi Dachi

An excellent defensive technique to protect
the head and neck.

Gyaku Shiho Kamae
Side View

Neko Ashi Dachi

Jodan Suihei Kamae
Upper Horizontal Stance

Zenkutsu Dachi

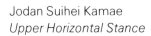

Upper block in the forward stance.

Upper block to defend the head and if
possible trap your opponents weapon.

Jodan Suihei Kamae
Upper Horizontal Stance

Hachiji Dachi Shizentai

Jodan Age Uke
Upper Rising Block

Kokutsu Dachi

A rising block to defend the centre line of
your body and especially the head.

Reversed rising block.

Jodan Gyaku Age Uke
Upper Reverse Rising Block

Kokutsu Dachi

Gedan Uke
Lower Block

Zenkutsu Dachi

A sweeping downward block to check or
deflect a low attack.

Held in the rear hand ready to strike, the
nunchaku are obscured from the opponents
sight.

Kakushi Gedan Kamae
Obscured Lower Stance

Zenkutsu Dachi

Gedan Ippon Uke
Lower Forearm Block

Kokutsu Dachi

The nunchaku is employed in protecting the
arm in this deflective block.

An effective counter to a diagonal attack to
the neck or head.

Ippon Soto Uke
Outside Forearm Block

Kokutsu Dachi

Juji Uke
X Block

Zenkutsu Dachi

The crossed nunchaku are used to block and
trap the attacking leg.

A frontal attack can be caught, and the
weapon forced from the opponent's hands.

Jodan Juji Uke
Upper X Block

Zenkutsu Dachi

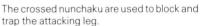

Sokumen Jodan Kamae
Upper Flank Stance

Zenkutsu Shizentai

An effective and flexible stance from which
to attack or defend.

Sokumen Jodan Kamae
Side View

Zenkutsu Shizentai

Dai Jodan Kamae
Upper Open Stance

Zenkutsu Dachi Shizentai

Allows you to strike with either hand to your
opponent's head or body.

Dai Jodan Kamae
Rear View

Zenkutsu Dachi Shizentai

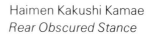
Haimen Kakushi Kamae
Rear Obscured Stance

Zenkutsu Dachi Shizentai

Partially obscured, the nunchaku is ready to
strike forwards in a wide arc.

Haimen Kakushi Dachi
Rear View

Zenkutsu Dachi Shizentai

25

Musubi Kamae
Entangled Stance

Zenkutsu Dachi Shizentai

With the arms wrapped around the body,
either hand can strike.

Musubi Kamae rear view of entangled
stance

Musubi Kamae
Rear View

Zenkutsu Dachi Shizentai

Itto Kamae
Sword Draw Stance

Zenkutsu Dachi

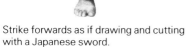

Strike forwards as if drawing and cutting
with a Japanese sword.

Itto Kamae
Side View

Zenkutsu Dachi

Ichi Monji Kamae
Upper Oblique Stance

Kokutsu Dachi

An effective defensive stance from which
retaliatory strikes can quickly be made.

Ichi Monji Kamae
Application

Kowaki Kamae
Under Arm Stance

Zenkutsu Dachi Shizentai

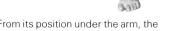

From its position under the arm, the
nunchaku is snapped forward to attack.

With the nunchaku over the shoulder grip
the free part under the arm from the rear.

Ura Kowaki Kamae
Reverse Under Arm Stance

Zenkutsu Dachi Shizentai

Morote Haimen Uke
Rear Defensive Block

Zenkutsu Dachi

An effective defensive stance to protect the head and back.

Morote Haimen Uke
Side View

Zenkutsu Dachi

Soku Men Gedan Uke
Lower Flank Block

Sagi Ashi Dachi

In 'crane' stance block downwards to stop
your opponent's attack.

To powerfully deflect an attack, strike
downwards and to the side.

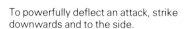

Soku Men Gedan Barai
Lower Flank Deflection

Sagi Ashi Dachi

Kubi Maki Kamae
Neck Encirclement Stance

Kokutsu Dachi

With the nunchaku wrapped around the neck, an attack can be launched from either side.

Rest the nunchaku on the shoulders and attack with either hand.

Kata Kake
Shoulder Position

Neko Ashi Dachi

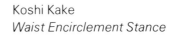

Koshi Kake
Waist Encirclement Stance

Neko Ashi Dachi

With the weapon partly hidden either hand
can strike.

Koshi Kake
Rear View

Neko Ashi Dachi

Morote Kamae
Double Nunchaku

Morote Kowaki Kamae
Double Under Arm Position

Kokutsu Dachi

In kokutsu dachi, the nunchaku are held under the arms ready to strike.

Double under arm stance performed in neko ashi dachi 'cat stance'.

Morote Kowaki Kamae
Double Under Arm Stance

Neko Ashi Dachi

Morote Muso Kamae
Double Nunchaku Shoulder Stance

Fudo Dachi

Hanging from the shoulders the nunchaku can quickly be snapped forward in a downward or circular attack.

Morote Muso Kamae
Rear View

Fudo Dachi

Nito Muso Kamae
Two Sword Shoulder Stance

Kokutsu Dachi

The forward arm parries while the other
holds the nunchaku ready to strike.

Nito Muso Kamae
Rear View

Kokutsu Dachi

Nito Kamae
Two Sword Stance

Kokutsu Dachi

The classical offensive/defensive position,
the left hand parries while the right attacks.

Stances

Rei No Kamae	Position for formal salutation, the weapon is held in the left hand signifying peaceful intent.
Yoi No Kamae	'Ready' position nunchaku in the right hand ready for use at any time.
Seigan No Kamae	'Facing the enemy stance' look into your opponents eyes.
Chudan Yama Kamae	The nunchaku are held in the shape of a mountain 'yama'.
Jodan Suihei Kamae	Upper horizontal guard stance, 'suihei' horizon.
Shiho Kamae	Four corners or square stance as in Aikido 'Shiho Nage'.
Gyaku Shiho Kamae	Reversed four corner stance.
Jodan Age Uke	'Jodan' upper 'Age' rising 'Uke' Block.
Jodan Gyaku Age Uke	Upper reversed rising block
Gedan Uke	Lower level block.
Kakushi Gedan Kamae	Similar to a technique from an old school of Japanese swordsmanship the weapon is obscured 'kakushi' so the enemy cannot judge its range.
Gedan Ippon Uke	Lower block using a single forearm.
Ippon Soto Uke	Single forearm outside block.
Juji Uke	'X' block from the Japanese character for ten 'Ju' which is written as a cross.
Jodan Juji Uke	Upper 'X' block.
Sokumen Jodan Kamae	The nunchaku is held against, and protects the flank.
Dai Jodan Kamae	Literally 'great upper stance', an open defensive position.
Haimen Kakushi Uchi	The nunchaku is held in an obscured position, 'kakushi' in the small of the back, 'haimen' so the the enemy cannot judge what technique will be used.
Musubi Kamae	The arms are wrapped around the body in the form of a knot 'musubi'.
Itto Kamae	The nunchaku is held in a sword drawing position.
Ichi Monji	Takes its name from the Japanese character for number one which is drawn as a horizontal line.
Kowaki Kamae	The free part of the nunchaku is held under the armpit 'kowaki'.

Stances

Ura Kowaki Kamae	Reverse under arm hold.
Morote Haimen Kamae	A classical defensive stance to protect the back 'haimen'.
Sokumen Gedan Uke	A downward block to protect the flank 'sokumen'.
Sokumen Gedan Barai	A downward deflective stroke protecting the flank.
Kubi Maki Kamae	Literally 'wrapped around the neck' position.
Kata Kake	Over the shoulders 'kake' stance.
Koshi Kake Kamae	The weapon is wrapped around the body at waist 'koshi' level.
Morote Kamae	Techniques employing two nunchaku.
Morote Kowaki Kamae	Double under arm position.
Morote Muso Kamae	A double nunchaku technique which effectively hides the weapons from the enemy.
Nito Muso Kamae	Taken from an old school of swordsmanship, the forward arm guards while the rear arm obscures the second weapon.
Nito Kamae	The favoured position of Japan's greatest swordsman Miyamoto Musashi the founder of the 'Nito' two sword school, which used the short sword (wakizashi) in the left hand and the long sword (katana) in the right.

Furi
Striking Techniques

1. Stand In Jodan Suihei Kamae   2. Begin to strike horizontally

Jodan Suihei Furi
Upper Horizontal Strike

Minimise the use of the elbow and
shoulder. Utilise the wrist to control the
movement of the baton in your hand,
and through it the other half of the
nunchaku.

3. Strike forwards and across the body   4. Retrieve with the free hand

1. Preparatory stance Ichimonji Kamae   2. Begin to strike

Jodan Inchimonji Furi
Upper Diagonal Strike

Keeping your forearm on the centre line,
strike downwards at 45 degrees.

Furi

3. Strike diagonally downwards sweeping upwards to return

4. Retrieve with the free hand

Application

Having blocked your opponents attack, strike him with ichimonji furi.

Dai Jodan Shajo Kaeshi
Upper Sloping Strike

'Dai Jodan' being the actual stance, and 'Shajo Kaeshi' being the technique. Cut forwards as far as possible in an arc as if using a sword, then bounce the nunchaku off your back to return it to the original position.

1. Preparatory stance Dai Jodan Kamae

4. Return the nunchaku around the body

2. Strike diagonally across the body   3. Continue the strike around the body

5. Sweep upwards and back   6. Catch the nunchaku behind your back
with the free hand

Morote Kote Gaeshi
From Itto no Kamae

Unlike 'Itto Kamae' the sword drawing technique when the nunchaku is swung forward in an arc, this technique relies on the 'snapping' action of the nunchaku pivoting around the joining cord or chain.

1. Preparatory stance Itto no Kamae

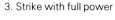

3. Strike with full power

2. Begin to strike

4. Continue striking with a wrist snapping
   action

Morote Kote Gaeshi
From Itto no Kamae

5. Retrieve the weapon with your left hand

7. Return to Itto No Kamae

6. Withdraw left hand

Morote Kote Gaeshi
From Yama Kamae

1. Stand in Yama Kamae

3. Strike with a wrist snapping action

2. Prepare to strike by withdrawing the left hand

4. Continue the technique to return the nunchaku

Morote Kote Gaeshi
From Yama Kamae

5. Catch the nunchaku with the left hand

6. Return to Yama Kamae

Kote Uchi Gaeshi
Snap Strike

The power for this technique is
generated by the 'snapping' action of
the wrist and elbow, while the correct
rotation of the forearm controls the
successful return of the nunchaku to the
receiving hand.

1. Preparatory stance

2. Ready to strike

3. Strike across the body   4. Return the nunchaku around the body

5. Retrieve the nunchaku in front of you   6. Return to Yama Kamae

1. Preparatory stance Sokumen Jodan Kamae

2. Strike diagonally across the body

3. Continue the strike returning the nunchaku around the body

4. Retrieve in front of you

Shajo Kote Gaeshi
From Sokumen Jodan Kamae

While similar to Kote Uchi Kaeshi, this
technique is much 'larger' and is
centred on the movement of the upper
arm and shoulder.

Kowaki Furi
Under Arm Strike

When performing this technique, cut
vertically downwards until the half way
point, then move your elbow out slightly
and use a slight flexing of the wrist to
return the nunchaku to an underarm
position.

1. Stand in Kowaki Kamae

2. Strike upwards and forwards

3. Continue the strike with full force

4. Raise the right arm in preparation for the retrieve

5. Catch the nunchaku under the arm

6. Return to Kowaki Kamae

1. Preparatory stance Ura Kowaki Kamae

2. Strike forwards in a large arc

3. Return the nunchaku upwards

Ura Kowaki Kaeshi
Reverse Under Arm Strike

Using the power of the wrist and elbow to strike downwards, and the whipping action at the bottom of the arc to return the nunchaku to the reverse underarm position.

Gyakute Hachiji Furi
Reverse Fig. 8 Strike

Exactly the same as the normal fig. 8
strike but with the gripping hand
reversed. Equal power is used on both
sides of the fig. 8, and maximum power
is applied when striking downwards at
45 degrees.

1. Preparatory stance Koshi Kake

2. With a reversed grip describe a wide arc
   to your right

3. Continue the strike downwards and to your left

4. Return the nuchaku across the body to complete the figure of eight

5. Return the nunchaku around the waist

6. Retrieve with the free hand and return to Koshi Kake

Ko Tsubame Gaeshi
Swallow Strike

From the stance shown, draw the nun-chaku from underneath, diagonally upwards across the body, then circling around the head. Strike downwards bouncing the nunchaku of the back to return them to the original position.

1. Preparatory stance Dai Jodan Kamae

2. Strike upwards across the body

3. And circling around the head . . .   4. Strike down again across the body

5. Return in front of the body   6. Retrieve and return to Dai Jodan Kamae

Morote Hachiji Furi
Double Fig. 8 Strike

Exactly the same technique as the single fig. 8 strike but when using two nunchaku, great care must be taken to synchronise them correctly so that they do not become tangled. From fig. 6 the technique changes to double reverse underarm strike.

1. Stand in Muso Kamae

2. Raise the arms and begin to strike

3. Strike forwards

4. Cross the arms in front of the body

5. Continue the swing upwards opening the arms to complete the figure eight strike

6. Retrieve the nunchaku in Morote Kowaki Kamae

7. Strike forwards and downwards

8. Change direction at the completion of the strike returning the nunchaku upwards

9. Prepare to retrieve

Strikes-Furi

Jodan Suihei Furi	Upper horizontal strike
Jodan Ichimonji Furi	Upper diagonal strike
Dai Jodan Shajo Kaeshi	Upper sloping strike and return
Morote Kote Gaeshi	Wrist snap strike and double handed return
Kote Uchi Gaeshi	Snap strike and return
Shajo Kote Gaeshi	Sloping wrist strike
Kowaki Furi	Under arm strike
Ura Kowaki Kaeshi	Reverse under arm strike
Gyakute Hachiji Furi	Reverse figure eight strike
Ko-tsubame Gaeshi	Swallow strike and return
Morote Hachiji Furi	Double figure eight strike
Morote Ura Waki Gaeshi	Double under arm strike

Bu Ho no Kata
Formal Exercise

Out of the centuries of war and conflict, emerged a social class so different from the rest of medieval Japanese society, as to be a race apart. Fiercely brave, intelligent and resourceful, the bushi, (bu-war shi-person) or samurai, with his martial skills and ability to disregard danger and death, was a formidable adversary.

It is the attributes of the samurai that we must cultivate if we wish to become skilled in the martial ways. There is of course no substitute for practice, but unless the skill so acquired is combined with determination and a sense of purpose, the peak of ability will never be reached.

Therefore, when you practice this fighting kata, you must concentrate on making your movements smooth and fluid like the flow of a great and powerful river. This fluidity of movement, which comes only from constant practice is the secret of the nunchaku's power. By harnessing it, you will be able to change smoothly and confidently from one technique to another, making it impossible for your opponent to guess your next move nor plan his own. Being unable either to judge the range of your weapon or with which hand you will strike next, he will quickly succumb to a well timed attack.

Bu Ho no Kata should be studied by all students once the basic techniques have been mastered. Its serious study is the key to the development of the speed, strength and skill that makes the nunchaku such a devastating weapon in expert hands. But remember, merely waving the nunchaku around, while it may impress your classmates and boost your ego, will not improve your technique. Rather, when you practice this kata, do as the samurai of ancient times did, and picture in your mind many adversaries attacking you. Defend yourself strongly, and counterattack with full power, putting your heart and soul into every movement. Do this, and eventually you will know the pleasure and satisfaction that mastery of Bu Ho no Kata can bring.

1. Ready stance change nunchaku to right hand after bowing.

2. Breathing in, slide the right leg forward and raise the nunchaku.

5. Perform a reversed rising block.

6. Step forward with the right foot and raise the nunchaku ready to perform . . . . . .

3. Breathing out, lower the nunchaku into the 'Seigan no Kamae'.

4. Slide the left foot back while breathing in and . . . . . .

7. A forward strike at high speed.

8. Slide back the left leg and at the same time perform a rising block at high speed.

9. Strike diagonally down across the body.

10. Bounce the nunchaku off the back and using the energy generated.

13. Start to perform a figure of eight strike.

14. Continue the figure of eight strike stepping forward with the left leg.

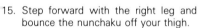

11. Return it over the shoulder and . . . . . .

12. Catch it in the left hand in the 'Dai Jodan Kamae' stance.

15. Step forward with the right leg and bounce the nunchaku off your thigh.

16. Using the whiplash effect, raise the nunchaku up.

17. Step backwards with the right foot.

18. Step back with the left foot and perform a diagonal cut.

21. Catching it behind with your left hand.

22. Swing up the left leg to start the next technique then raise the nunchaku and jump at the same time.

19. Follow through allowing the nunchaku to circle the waist.

20. Then rebound it upwards across the body . . . . . .

23. As you land on the left foot withdraw the right leg and simultaneously strike with the left hand.

24. Completion of 'O Tsubame gaeshi' technique.

25. Step backwards with the right foot.   26. Turn and perform a horizontal strike.

29. Strike strongly downwards at the side   30. Swinging upwards along the same line
     of the body.   and catch with the right hand.

27. Continue to swing back.

28. Start to swing upwards ready to per-
    form the next technique.

31. Using the right hand swing the nun-
    chaku across front of the body over
    the right shoulder and catch with the
    left hand.

32. Perform an upper horizontal block.

33. Sliding the right foot forward perform an 'X' block.

34. Raise the nunchaku and perform an upper horizontal block.

37. Complete the turn by pivoting on the balls of the feet and strike to the right with a figure of eight strike.

38. Bounce the nunchaku off the back after completing the fig 8 strike . . . . . .

35. Slide back the left foot into 'kokutsu dachi' stance and slowly perform a 'square' block.

36. Turn to the right moving the left leg forward and turning the nunchaku around the head.

39. And swinging it diagonally up across the body . . . . . .

40. Continue the swing over the shoulder and catch with the left hand.

41. Step to the left with the left foot.

42. Turn 90 degrees to your right and perform a fig 8 strike.

45. Swing the nunchaku and the left leg up simultaneously . . . . . .

46. Turn clockwise sliding the left leg backwards and strike with the left hand.

43. Continue the fig 8 strike.

44. Return the nunchaku over the right shoulder and catch with the left hand.

47. Swing the nunchaku back over the left shoulder . . . . . .

48. And catch behind the back with the right hand.

49. Raise the nunchaku ready to strike.

50. Strike downwards and to your left.

53. Step to the front with the right foot raising the nunchaku over your head . . . . . .

54. And strike downwards to your left with a diagonal strike.

51. Continue the fig 8 strike . . . . . .

52. Returning the nunchaku over the shoulder to be caught with the right hand.

55. Returning upwards and over the right shoulder to be caught by the right hand.

56. Step forward with the right leg striking upwards with the right hand . . . . . .

57. And returning it over the right shoulder to be caught with the left hand.

58. Strike downwards to the right . . . . . .

61. Returning the nunchaku over the left shoulder to be caught with the right hand.

62. Start to perform a fig 8 strike.

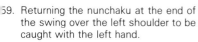

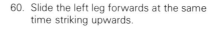

59. Returning the nunchaku at the end of the swing over the left shoulder to be caught with the left hand.

60. Slide the left leg forwards at the same time striking upwards.

63. Continue fig 8 strike stepping forward.

64. Fig 8 strike ends as right leg reaches the correction position of 'zenkutsu dachi' stance.

65. Step forward with the left leg as you swing the nunchaku around your thigh.

66. Start to perform a complete circle with the nunchaku in front of you.

69. Returning the nunchaku on completion over the left shoulder to be caught by the right hand.

70. Swing up the right leg and nunchaku in preparation for jumping . . . . . .

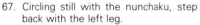

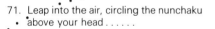

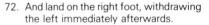

67. Circling still with the nunchaku, step back with the left leg.

68. Step back with the right foot and execute a diagonal strike . . . . . .

71. Leap into the air, circling the nunchaku above your head . . . . . .

72. And land on the right foot, withdrawing the left immediately afterwards.

73. Swing the nunchaku around the back in unison with the movement of the left leg, then stepping to the front with the left leg.

74. Pivot on the balls of the feet to face the front and execute a mid level horizontal strike.

77. Returning the nunchaku upwards at the bottom of the arc......

78. And over the shoulder to be caught with the left hand.

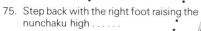

75. Step back with the right foot raising the nunchaku high . . . . . .

76. Then strike downwards strongly . . . . . .

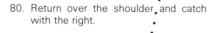

79. Swing upwards in front of the body with the left hand . . . . . .

80. Return over the shoulder and catch with the right.

81. Bring the nunchaku to the front guard position . . . . . .

82. And prepare to raise it into . . . . . .

85. Raise it slowly to the middle position . . . . . .

86. Then snap upwards to perform a powerful upper horizontal block.

83. The upper horizontal block position.

84. Execute an 'X' block to the front.

87. Strike with an upper horizontal strike . . . . . .

88. And catch the nunchaku in the left hand.

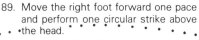
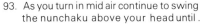

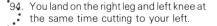

89. Move the right foot forward one pace and perform one circular strike above the head.

90. Step forward with the left leg and perform one more circular strike.

93. As you turn in mid air continue to swing the nunchaku above your head until . .

94. You land on the right leg and left knee at the same time cutting to your left.

91. Step forward with the right leg.

92. Swinging the nunchaku strongly above the head, leap off of the left foot.

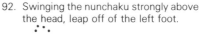
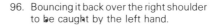

95. Return the nunchaku around the waist.

96. Bouncing it back over the right shoulder to be caught by the left hand.

97

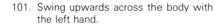

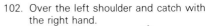

97. Stand up and perform a fig 8 strike.

98. Withdraw your right foot close to your left . . . . . .

101. Swing upwards across the body with the left hand.

102. Over the left shoulder and catch with the right hand.

99. And strike strongly downwards at the side of the body . . . . . .

100. Swinging back over the right shoulder and catching with the left hand.

103. Move your right leg to the side.

104. Then perform an upper horizontal block.

105. Bring your feet together, nunchaku in front of the body.

106. Adopt the formal position, ready for the bow.

Bu Ho no Kata
Applications

1. Face your opponent in Seigan no Kamae.

2. As your opponent strikes at your head, block with Gyaku age uke using the power of your hips to make the block more effective.

3. His attack temporarily checked, swing the nunchaku backwards and strike downwards at his ribs or hip.

1. Block with Gyaku age uke, reversed rising block.

2. At the instant of contact give way to the right to unbalance your opponent and diverting his attack.

3. Immediately strike his head while maintaining your guard with the left hand.

1. Stop your opponent's attack with Age uke rising block.

2. At the instant that his momentum is lost start to strike forwards.

3. Continue your attack striking your opponent on the head, neck or shoulder.

1. Block with Age uke rising block.

2. Strike downwards wrapping the nunchaku around your thigh.

3. Unwind the nunchaku, and as it accelerates swing it upwards and over your opponent's weapon.

4. With the attacker's weapon under control, launch your counter-attack.

1. Block with Age uke rising block.

2. Strike downwards to encircle your thigh with the nunchaku

3. Bouncing the nunchaku off the thigh, swing it over the attacker's weapon and immobilise it by grasping the second baton.

4. Counter attack with Mae geri, front kick, to your opponent's face.

1. Stand in Sokumen jodan kamae.

2. Block with Jodan suihei uke, upper horizontal block.

3. Catch the attacker's weapon, and force it down.

5. Pre-empt the second attack by striking Juji zuki to your opponent's throat.

4. If your opponent escapes, withdraw quickly.

1. Block an attack to your side with Ippon uchi uke.

3. Control your opponents weapon by grasping the hilt and strike to his neck or head
   with your free hand.

2. Divert the force of the attack unbalancing your opponent.

1. Face your opponent in Musubi dachi with the arms wrapped around the body.

3. Then without hesitating strike downwards diagonally to your opponent's head or neck.

2. Draw with the right hand and sweep upwards in a wide arc to force him back.

1. Standing in Dai Jodan Kamae, your opponent threatens you with a knife.

2. Draw with your left hand and strike at his wrist.

3. Before he can recover, step forward and strike him strongly behind the knee.

1. Against a horizontal attack block with Ippon soto uke.

2. Step inside and strike to the attacker's chest.

1. Block a low level horizontal attack to your side with Ippon gedan uke.

2. Before he regains his balance, step forward and strike with the butt of the nunchaku.

1. In a close combat situation strike with the butt of the nunchaku.

2. Follow with Nodowa juji zuki to the throat with the ends of the nunchaku crossed over.

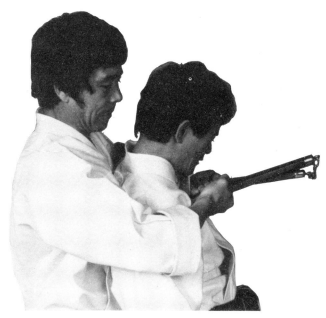

1. Grasping your opponent from behind strike him in the chest with the butts of both nunchaku.

2. Stepping backwards slightly, subdue him with a reverse stranglehold.

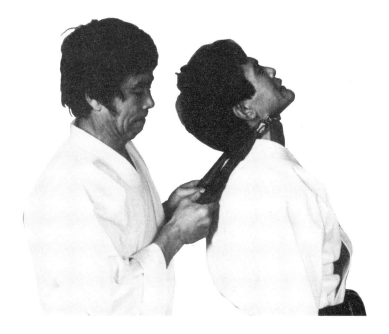

1. Subdue a direct frontal attack by trapping the antagonist's arm in the nunchaku chain or cord.

2. Wrap the chain around his arm, at the same time stepping forwards and force your opponent backwards and to your left.

1a. This rear view shows how the attacking arm is entangled in the cord or chain.

2a. Force your opponent backwards and to your left to unbalance him and prevent a
further attack with his left hand.

1. Grasp the attacking arm.

2. Crossing the nunchaku chains beneath his arm, swing him to the side to break his balance.

1. To defend against a front kick strike your opponent's shin before his attack reaches full power.

2. Without hesitating, step to the side wrapping the chain around his leg and throw him to the floor.

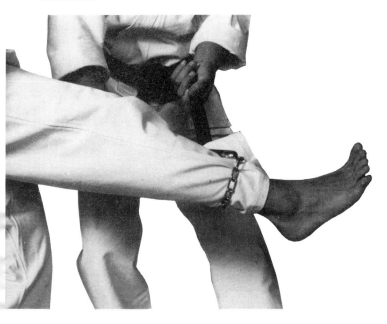

1. Block an attack to the head with Ichi monji uke.

3. Encircle the wrist completely taking advantage of your opponent's retreat to unbalance him

2. Without pausing, wrap the chain around your opponent's wrist.

4. Apply pressure to the completed lock and stepping forward force your attacker down.

1a. An instant before your opponent makes contact, lunge forward and strike him in the groin.

May I take this opportunity to remind students that these additional striking techniques should not be practised, as even under controlled conditions, serious injuries can result. They are only included here as a reference to ancient practice.

In some parts of the world, the use of nunchaku and related Kobudo weapons is forbidden by law, and even possession could lead to arrest and prosecution for possession of an offensive weapon. Even where their use is allowed, I urge students to demonstrate the responsible attitude that is stressed in martial arts training, by carrying them in a suitable case, preferably wrapped up in your training clothes and carried in an equipment bag or holdall, and *never* ready for use, or concealed about the person.

The responsibility to protect the legacy of the ancient masters of the martial arts rests upon the shoulders of us all. One rash or inconsiderate act can easily destroy the efforts of the many instructors who have striven to make these ancient arts acceptable to the public at large.

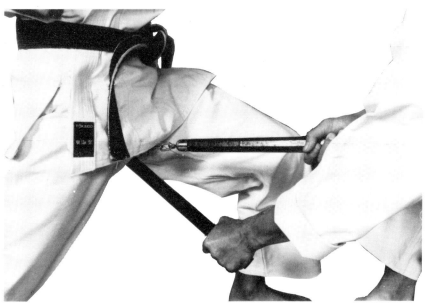

Detail of Fig. 1a. left

Strike to the stomach with the butt of the nunchaku.

Using the length of the nunchaku to outdistance him, strike your opponent on both sides of his head.

The eyes are vulnerable to this double-handed attack.

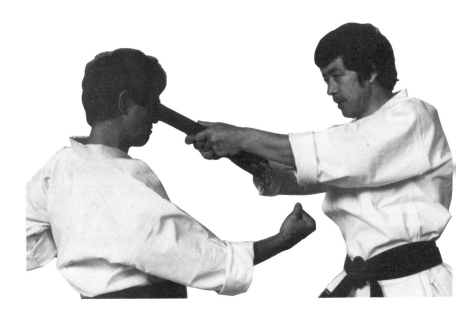

Prevent your opponent from completing his attack by striking his wrist strongly.

Drop below his attack and strike your opponent in the ribs with the butts of both nunchaku.

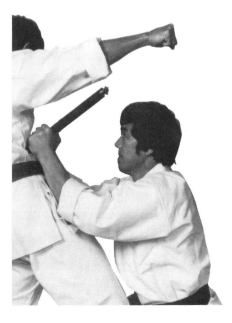

Ju Ho no Kata
Health Method Exercise

Woodblock print of Samurai figures by Kuniyoshi.

As the Bu Ho no Kata was developed to be a fighting exercise, creating in its lightning movements a seemingly inpenetrable defence and irresistible attack, so Ju Ho no Kata was created to be performed for the benefit of mind and body.

Practising Ju Ho no Kata, literally 'health method exercise' improves bodily functions, increases energy levels and relieves muscular pain and stiffness so often experienced by students of Karate-Do. It achieves this by uniquely combining a set of balanced and fluid movements designed to flex and strengthen the muscles, with the stimulation of certain nerve points in a manner similar to that used in acupuncture and oriental therapeutic massage.

As the principles upon which the movements of this exercise are based are largely unknown in the West, it may help the reader to understand something of Oriental medicine before proceeding with the exercise.

A fundamental principle of Oriental medicine is that life force or energy, ch'i (Ki in Japanese), is constantly moving around the body along fixed routes or meridians. This energy is composed of opposite but complementary forces, Yin the negative and Yang the positive, much as an electrical current is. As with a current of electricity one can never exist without the other. At birth we are all endowed with a certain amount of ch'i (for the total absence of ch'i is equivalent to the total absence of life) and it ebbs as we labour and use energy, and flows and increases as we eat, drink and breathe. This force in a healthy body is in a state of perfect balance, Yin equals Yang exactly and ch'i flows along its pathways or meridians and all is well. But when an inbalance occurs and the two polar forces of Yin and Yang do not match each other, remedial action must be swiftly taken if the body is not to suffer ill health.

In the Orient, and increasingly in the West as well, many people resort to one of the most effective treatments for this imbalance, namely acupuncture or one of the associated therapies. An ancient medical skill of the Chinese, pre-dating the birth of the Christian era by more than two thousand years, our earliest reference to it is to be found in the 'Nei Ching' or Classic of Internal Medicine attributed to the emperor Huang Ti (The Yellow Emperor 2697-2586 B.C.) This text, still in use today, forms the basis from which modern acupuncture has been developed over the past forty centuries.

Simply expressed, acupuncture seeks to restore the natural flow of life force in the correct quantity and balance so that good health returns as a result. It achieves this end by stimulating specific points which lie along the meridians by inserting needles as in acupuncture, massage, 'shiatsu' or by the use of heat 'moxibustion' The latter, which involves the burning of moxa, small pieces of wormwood (Artemisia vulgaris) either directly on acupuncture points, or on the end of needles inserted into them, is particularly popular in Japan where the moist climate makes it especially effective in the relief of muscular or internal pain and the generation of energy.

If the diagnosis of the inbalance was correct, and the treatment properly applied, the balance of the polar forces will be restored, ch'i will again flow as nature intended and good health will be restored. This concept of the balance of Yin and Yang is fundamental to other aspects of Chinese culture

Woodblock print of Mt. Fuji

such as art and literature as well as the practice of medicine. Yin the negative and feminine force is associated with cold and dark things, the moon, water and the earth, and the Yang, positive masculine force with warmth, the sun and sky. Constantly reacting with each other, and unable to exist in isolation they are depicted in the ancient Chinese Yin Yang sign as being at once opposed, yet made inseparable by the inclusion of part of each within the other.

When we practice the Ju Ho no Kata, it is with this concept of the balance of

by the 19th century artist Hokusai.

Yin and Yang in mind. The movements are balanced and fluid, they exercise the body fully. At certain points in the exercise we strike specific acupunc-

ture points to stimulate them and bring about relief from pain, stiffness and other common conditions. At the end of each section we return to the beginning and perform it again on the other side, i.e. starting with the opposite hand so as to be in a state of complete equilibrium before moving onto the next section of the exercise.

Divided into four sections, each designed to exercise particular parts of the body and stimulate specific meridians, the exercise is performed in the following logical sequence.

Isetsu (part 1) Strikes to the shoulder and neck to relieve head and shoulder aches and clear the head.

Nisetsu (part 2) Strikes to lower and upper back to relieve back pain and gastric disorders.

Sansetsu (part 3) Strikes to lower and upper back, for stiffness and back pain.

Yonsetsu (part 4) Strikes to upper arm, ankle, rear of knees and back to improve joint movement, relieve stomach pain, aid weight loss and improve respiration.

To enhance the balance and fluidity of the movements, and emphasise the health rather than military aspects of this exercise, Ju Ho no Kata can be performed to a suitable musical accompaniment which creates a pleasing rhythm, and endowes the movements with a dignity and grace not associated with purely physical regimes. Particularly suited to the more mature student this unique system of exercise should be of practical benefit to all who study it.

● *Signifies Nerve Point Strike*

1. Starting Position in 'musubi kamae'.

2. Commence a reverse fig 8 strike.

● 5. Strike your shoulder.

6. Before retrieving it with your left hand.

3. Continue fig 8 strike.

4. And returning the nunchaku around your back . . .

7. Draw with the right hand and strike downwards returning the nunchaku upwards at the bottom of the arc . . .

● 8. Returning the nunchaku to be caught in the left hand after striking the back.

9. Draw with the left hand returning the nunchaku over the shoulder . . .

●10. To strike the back again. Draw with the left hand . . .

●13. Swing around the back to encircle the neck with the chain.

14. And catch with the left hand.

11. And perform another back strike retrieving the nunchaku with the right hand.

12. Draw with the left hand, and circling the nunchaku in front of you . . .

15. Draw with the left hand and striking across the body to your right . . .

16. Catch in 'musubi dachi' and return to fig 1 repeating the whole of 'isetsu' with the other hand.

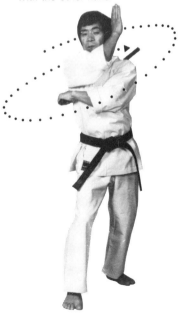

17. At the end of each of the four sections of
     Ju Ho no Kata, the performer returns to
     the beginning of the section that he has
     just completed and performs it again on
     the 'other side'. For example, in the
     case of 'Isetsu' this means returning
     from Fig. 17 on this page, to Fig. 1 and
     starting the section again by drawing
     with the right hand. On reaching Fig. 17
     again you begin the second section
     'Nisetsu'.

1. Nisetsu begins with 'dai jodan kamae'.

2. Swing the right leg and the nunchaku up at the same time, and turning anti-clockwise . . .

3. Strike in a wide arc in front of you . . .

4. Bouncing the nunchaku off the back.

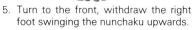

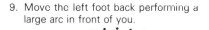

5. Turn to the front, withdraw the right foot swinging the nunchaku upwards.

6. Swing down in a large arc sliding the right foot forwards.

9. Move the left foot back performing a large arc in front of you.

•10. Bounce the nunchaku off your back and return it over your right shoulder to be caught by the left hand.

7. And strike the back of the thigh with 'komata gaeshi'.

8. Bouncing the nunchaku upwards, withdraw the right foot.

11. Draw with the left hand and returning to fig 2 perform 'tsubame gaeshi' to start the reverse sequence of 'nisetsu'.

Fig. 11 is the reverse of Fig. 1, so restart
this section from Fig. 2 and perform on
the other side. On reaching Fig. 11 for
the second time, perform Jodan Suihei
Kamae ready to start section three
Sansetsu.

1. Starting position.

2. Raise the right hand and turning to the left . . .

3. Swing down across the body striking the hips . . .

● 4. And return upwards to strike the upper arm.

- 5. Strike the hips again.

6. And retrieve the nunchaku in front of the body.

- 9. Strike the back at waist level . . .

- 10. Returning upwards to strike the back at chest level.

7. Turn to the front . . .

8. And taking up the 'sokumen jodan kamae' position . . .

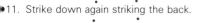

11. Strike down again striking the back.

12. And controlling the nunchaku with the right hand . . .

13. Retrieve in front of the body with the left.

15. End of reverse sequence.

14. Raising the left arm, turn to the right and begin the reverse sequence from 'sansetsu' fig 3.

Start Sansetsu again from Fig. 14 by returning to Fig. 3 and performing the whole section again on the other side. On reaching Fig. 14 for the second time, perform Jodan Suihei Kamae Fig. 15, ready to start Yonsetsu.

1. Start in 'sokumen jodan kamae'.

2. Using the wrist, swing the nunchaku forward . . .

3. And strike the arm above the elbow.

- 4. Swing the right leg up at the same time wrapping the chain around the lower leg.

  8. Pivot on the balls of the feet moving the right foot across swinging the nunchaku upwards.

- 5. Bounce the nunchaku off the leg and swing round to strike behind the knees.

  9. Continue the swing over the shoulder and catch with the right hand, return to fig 2 to start reverse sequence.

6. Bounce the nunchaku off the back of the knees and catch behind the waist.

● 7. Slide the left leg forward and drawing with the left hand.

10. Finishing position of kata.

From Fig. 9 which is the reverse of Yonsetsu Fig. 1 perform this section again on the other side starting from Fig. 2. Finish on Fig. 10 to complete the whole of the Ju Ho no Kata, Health Method Exercise.

Other Titles published by Dragon Books

Advanced Shotokan Kata Series
By Keinosuke Enoeda 8th Dan

Volume 1
Bassai-Dai : Kanku-Dai : Jion : Empi : Hangetsu

Volume 2
Bassai-sho : Kanku-sho : Jiin : Gankaku : Sochin

Volume 3
Tekki-Nidan : Tekki-Sandan *(2 versions)* : Nijushiho
: Gojushiho-Dai : Gojushiho-sho *(in preparation)*

Shadow of the Ninja
By Katsumi Toda

Revenge of the Shogun's Ninja
By Katsumi Toda

Kubotan Keychain – Instrument of Attitude Adjustment
By Takayuki Kubota 8th Dan

The Ninja Star – Art of Shuriken Jutsu
By Katsumi Toda

Balisong – Iron Butterfly
By C. Hernandez (in preparation)

Ninja Death Vow
By Katsumi Toda (in preparation)

The Police Baton – A Manual for Law Enforcement Officers
By Takayuki Kubota 8th Dan (in preparation)

Sakura Dragon Corporation
P.O. Box 6039 Thousand Oaks
California 91359 USA.